A Gift For:

From:

Editorial Director: Carrie Bolin
Editor: Lindsay Evans
Art Director: Chris Opheim
Designer: Mary Eakin
Production Designer: Bryan Ring
Lettering Artist: Amber Goodvin

ISBN: 978-1-59530-712-5
1BOK2173

Made in China
0617

I believe in you
and the things
that are important
to you...

because you're important to me.

I Believe

You Truly make a

difference...

JUST BY BEING YOU.

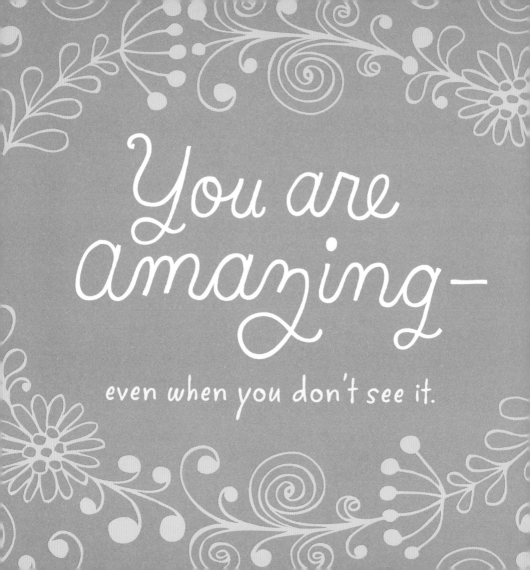

(Trust me on this one. OK?)

I BELIEVE YOU'RE

A FORCE FOR GOOD.

Look out, forces of evil!
Good is gonna show you the door.

I BELIEVE YOU WERE PUT IN MY liFE FOR A REASON.

AND THAT
blesses me
EVERY DAY.

You shape others in little ways

(AND BIG ONES).

YOU AMAZE.
You inspire.

And you do *sleep*, don't you?!

I BELIEVE

YOU ARE
A NINJA OF NICE—
always doing a little covert kindness.

You're a giver.

AND I'VE BEEN
lucky ENOUGH
TO BE ON THE
RECEIVING END OF
YOUR GIVING.

I Believe

YOU *L*OVELY *U*P EVERY DAY.

YOU ARE A
TRUE Gift TO THE WORLD,
AND THE WORLD
NEEDS YOU JUST THE
WAY YOU ARE.

So don't
ever change,
OK?

I Believe

YOUR PRESENCE MAKES

everything BETTER.

In that way,
you're kind of
like bacon.

I believe you have what it takes
to face the tough stuff

and to grow from every experience
life brings your way.

THERE'S A
STRENGTH IN YOU,
A LIGHT IN YOU,

NO ONE COULD EVER

DULL YOUR SPARKLE.

I BELIEVE
happiness
FOLLOWS YOU

LIKE A STAMPEDE OF PUPPIES...
and that's not a coincidence.

You make the world
a better place just by
being in it.

YOU'RE DISTINCTLY, authentically YOU...

NOT A VERSION OF SOMEONE ELSE.

And I love that about you.

I Believe You Have a Glow That Comes From the Inside.

And not in a creepy
sci-fi kind of way.

Your presence can change lives.

It's already changed mine.

I BELIEVE YOU'RE ONE OF THOSE PEOPLE WHO JUST INNATELY LiFTS PEOPLE'S *spirits.*

You're like the human equivalent
of caffeine.

YOU ADD A BiG OL'

TO LiFE.

I love the excitement
and fun that you bring
to ordinary days.

I believe in you...

AND YOUR ABILITY TO TAKE THE UNEXPECTED AND MAKE IT INTO SOMETHING unbelievably GOOD.

YOU **C**AN DO
anything
YOU SET OUT
TO ACCOMPLISH.

Except wash a new
red shirt with a load
of whites.

I Believe You Are

ONE OF THE RARITIES.

You have a caring heart, and somehow, you don't let the stresses of life today change that about you.

YOU LISTEN, really listen-

and not just wait for your turn
to speak.

I Believe
You are an example.

Of course you are—
look how many times you've
inspired me!

I **B**ELIEVE
YOU NEVER GET HOW
awesome
YOU ARE,

which makes you that much
more awesome.

If we were desserts on
a dessert cart, you'd be the
one everyone pointed at and
went "oooooh."

simply because I know you.

I Believe
You must have a
Superhero cape tucked
away somewhere.

You really know
how to save the day.

If You shine

ANY BRIGHTER,

You'll Glow
in the Dark.

I BELIEVE
THE WORLD NEEDS YOU
JUST THE WAY
YOU ARE.

You're great
at being you.

And that makes me want
to be a better me.

I BELIEVE THE REALLY GREAT THING ABOUT YOU IS everything ABOUT YOU.

IF YOU LOOKED UP "WONDERFUL" IN THE DICTIONARY,

you'd find a terrible picture of you.
I drew it.

I Believe You're an Inspiration...

even on your worst of days.

We're all a part of something
bigger than ourselves...

AND I KNOW
IT'S SOMETHING
beautiful,
BECAUSE I'VE SEEN
IT IN YOU.

I Believe

YOU ADD KINDNESS
TO THE WORLD.

I Believe that on any Given Day, Most of the Smiles I See can Be Traced

BACK TO YOU.

There's good, there's great,
there's canned squirty cheese,
and then there's you.

You make life so much better.

YOU'RE
outstanding...

EVEN WHEN YOU'RE
NOT STANDING OUTSIDE.

I BELIEVE
IN THE MAGIC OF
ALL THAT YOU ARE.

And that's you.

I Believe
In Your Goodness.

If you have enjoyed this book
or it has touched your life in some way,
we would love to hear from you.

Please send your comments to:
Hallmark Book Feedback
P.O. Box 419034
Mail Drop 100
Kansas City, MO 64141

Or e-mail us at:
booknotes@hallmark.com